BRACKETIVITY
HOLIDAY

You Decide Who Wins!

By Cala Spinner

Andrews McMeel
PUBLISHING®

Andrews McMeel Publishing
a division of Andrews McMeel Universal
1130 Walnut Street, Kansas City, Missouri 64106

www.andrewsmcmeel.com

23 24 25 26 27 RLP 10 9 8 7 6 5 4 3 2 1

ISBN: 978-1-5248-8595-3

Editor: Erinn Pascal
Art Director: Tiffany Meairs
Production Editor: Meg Utz
Production Manager: Tamara Haus

Made by:
Shenzhen Reliance Printing Co., Ltd.
Address and place of manufacturer:
25 Longshan Industrial Zone, Nanling,
Longgang District, Shenzhen, China, 518114
1st Printing – 5/15/23

ATTENTION: SCHOOLS AND BUSINESSES

BRACKETIVITY
HOLIDAY

Ho, ho, ho! It's that special time of year—the holidays! There's a certain air in this time of year that's just so great. Perhaps it's the hustle and bustle of the mall, the chimes of Christmas bells, the flicker of Hanukkah lights, or the fact that everyone's in the holiday spirit.

Of course, there's many things to debate, too! What's the best stocking stuffer—headphones or a candle? Arts and crafts supplies or trading cards? Funky jewelry or a hot chocolate kit?

In your hands (or your *mittens*) is a very special holiday-themed **Bracketivity** book. Within these pages, you'll be able to pick your favorite "thing" in each category. But it's not just a "pick and go" situation—you'll have to fill each bracket to determine your winner!

Think about each answer carefully because it determines your next round of **brackets**. Or go with your gut feeling—really, there's no wrong answers! And at the end of the book, you'll even get to make your own **Bracketivities** to share with family and friends.

Just remember—have fun! You decide who wins.

What's the best stocking stuffer?

Warm Socks

Candy — **Candy**

Stickers

New Book — **New Book**

Candy (Warm Socks / Candy vs Stickers / New Book → Candy)

Headphones

Candle — **Candle**

Arts and Crafts Supplies — **Arts and Crafts Supplies**

Trading Cards

Arts and Crafts Supplies

Candy (Candy vs Arts and Crafts Supplies → Candy)

BRACKETIVITY EXAMPLE

Here's an example **Bracketivity** that's filled out. It's what your author would pick. Don't worry—if you disagree, you'll get to fill out your own on the next page.

Knitted Hat

Slippers — **Slippers**

Nail Polish

Nail Polish — **Nail Polish**

Tennis Balls

Slippers (Knitted Hat / Slippers vs Nail Polish / Tennis Balls → Slippers)

Sunglasses

Sheet Mask — **Sheet Mask**

Planner

Planner — **Planner**

Lip Scrub

Sheet Mask

Slippers

Candy

Comic Books

Comic Books — Winner

Mittens — **Mittens**

Dice

Chocolate — **Chocolate**

Bubbles

Chocolate

Fidget Toy

Bath Soap — **Bath Soap**

Sidewalk Chalk

Money — **Money**

Money

Money

Comic Books — **Comic Books**

Tarot Deck

Hot Sauce — **Hot Sauce**

Stuffed Animal

Comic Books

Funky Jewelry — **Funky Jewelry**

Hot Cocoa Kit

Funny Mug

Hair Clip — **Hair Clip**

Hair Clip

Hair Clip

Comic Books

What's the best stocking stuffer?

Warm Socks

Candy

Stickers

New Book

Headphones

Candle

Arts and Crafts Supplies

Trading Cards

Knitted Hat

Slippers

Nail Polish

Tennis Balls

Sunglasses

Sheet Mask

Planner

Lip Scrub

Winner

Mittens

Dice

Chocolate

Bubbles

Fidget Toy

Bath Soap

Sidewalk Chalk

Money

Comic Books

Tarot Deck

Hot Sauce

Stuffed Animal

Funky Jewelry

Hot Cocoa Kit

Funny Mug

Hair Clip

What's the best thing to do on Christmas Eve?

Give Gifts

Wait for Santa Claus

Go Ice-Skating

Watch Christmas Movies on TV

Bake Cookies

Go to Church

Sleep In Late

Spend Time with Family

Perform in a Christmas Play

Go to the Movies

Go Christmas Caroling

Do Volunteer Work

Take Photos

Decorate the Christmas Tree

Make Christmas Dinner

Eat Christmas Dinner

Open Presents

Decorate a Gingerbread House

Read Christmas Stories

Go Sledding

Visit Another Place

Make a Christmas Ornament

Hang Christmas Lights

Curl Up by the Fire

Go (Last-Minute) Christmas Shopping

Have a Snowball Fight

Wrap Presents

Host a Christmas Party

Build a Snowperson

Attend a Tree-Lighting Ceremony

Wear Ugly Christmas Sweaters

Play Board Games

Winner

What's the best holiday food?

Eggnog

Peppermint Bark

Mashed Potatoes

Baked Ham

Sugar Cookies

Cheese Board

Mixed Nuts

Fish

Candy Canes

Chocolate Fudge

Sticky Toffee Pudding

Sweet Potato Pie

Custard

Cranberry Sauce

Roast Turkey

Fruitcake

Dinner Rolls

Baked Brie

Gingerbread Cookies

Cinnamon Rolls

Box of Chocolates

Red Velvet Cake

Stuffing

Beef Wellington

Pigs in Blankets

Potato Salad

Lasagna

Mac and Cheese

Scrambled Eggs

Crepes

Apple Pie

Doughnuts

Winner

What's the best holiday film?

How the Grinch Stole Christmas

Noelle

The Nutcracker

A Muppet Family Christmas

Gremlins

Home Alone

Frosty the Snowman

A Charlie Brown Christmas

Rudolph the Red-Nosed Reindeer

Miracle on 34th Street

Klaus

Santa Paws

The Dog Who Saved Christmas

Jingle All the Way

A Christmas Carol

Mickey's Once Upon a Christmas

The Polar Express

The Nightmare Before Christmas

Harry Potter and the Sorcerer's Stone

Christmas with the Kranks

Santa Claus is Coming to Town

It's a Wonderful Life

The Santa Clause

Prancer

Angela's Christmas

Jingle Jangle

Jack Frost

Elf

Deck the Halls

The Star

Elliott: The Littlest Reindeer

Arthur Christmas

Winner

Write in your own:

With the following prompt, fill in your own bracketivity!

Which of your friends or family members loves the holidays the MOST? You can even include yourself!!

Winner

What's the best holiday song?

"Santa Tell Me"

"Blue Christmas"

"All I Want for Christmas is You"

"Last Christmas"

"Rockin' Around the Christmas Tree"

"Rudolph the Red-Nosed Reindeer"

"Santa Claus is Coming to Town"

"Wonderful Christmastime"

"Dreidel, Dreidel, Dreidel"

"Jingle Bell Rock"

"It's the Most Wonderful Time of the Year"

"Frosty the Snowman"

"We Wish You a Merry Christmas"

"Silent Night"

"The Little Drummer Boy"

"Feliz Navidad"

"Have Yourself a Merry Little Christmas"

"You're a Mean One, Mr. Grinch"

"Let it Snow! Let it Snow! Let it Snow!"

"Twelve Days of Christmas"

"O Holy Night"

"I'll Be Home for Christmas"

"Puppy for Hanukkah"

"Please Come Home for Christmas"

"Grandma Got Run Over by a Reindeer"

"All I Want for Christmas (Is My Two Front Teeth)"

"(Everybody's Waitin' for) The Man with the Bag"

"My Only Wish (This Year)"

"Baby It's Cold Outside"

"Winter Wonderland"

"Jingle Bells"

"O Come, All Ye Faithful"

Winner

Santa loves cookies! Which cookie is your favorite?

Gingerbread

Snickerdoodle

Chocolate Peppermint

Ginger Honey Snap

Chocolate Crinkle

Peanut Butter

Oatmeal Raisin

Mint Chocolate

Lemon

Rainbow Sprinkle

Raspberry Thumbprint

Black and White

White Chocolate Macadamia

Sugar

Key Lime

Carrot Cake

Chocolate Chip

Double Chocolate

White Chocolate Strawberry

Butter Pecan

Cookies and Cream

Cherry Almond Shortbread

Salted Caramel

Red Velvet

Chocolate Turtle

Maple Pecan

Frosted Toffee

Pumpkin

Orange Creamsicle

Toasted Marshmallow

Butter

Rainbow

Winner

Of these places, where would you MOST want to celebrate the holidays?

Miami, Florida

New York City, New York

New Orleans, Louisiana

Montreal, Canada

London, United Kingdom

Cairo, Egypt

Rome, Italy

Maui, Hawaii

Cancún, Mexico

Istanbul, Turkey

Bali, Indonesia

Tokyo, Japan

Marrakesh, Morocco

Machu Picchu, Peru

Niagara Falls, New York

Hong Kong, China

Paris, France

Los Angeles, California

Venice, Italy

North Pole, Alaska

Boston, Massachusetts

Basel, Switzerland

Edinburgh, Scotland

Vienna, Austria

Vatican City

Amsterdam, Netherlands

Dublin, Ireland

Berlin, Germany

Las Vegas, Nevada

Bethlehem, West Bank

Sydney, Australia

Beijing, China

Winner

Santa has eight reindeer. But what if he had eight different animals? Which animal would be the best replacement?

Blue Whales

Lions

Mountain Goats

Red Pandas

Frogs

Snakes

Wolves

Horses

Camels

Pelicans

Hippopotamuses

Elephants

Cheetahs

Cows

Deer

Swans

Tigers

Giraffes

Unicorns

Dogs

Axolotls

Koalas

Capybaras

Dinosaurs

Turtles

Sheep

Meerkats

Sloths

Donkeys

Grizzly Bears

Hedgehogs

Bats

Winner

What's your favorite celebration?

Kwanzaa

New Year's Eve

April Fool's Day

Eid al-Adha

Holi

Thanksgiving

Father's Day

Easter

Ramadan

Lunar New Year

Independence Day

Mardi Gras

Christmas

Diwali

Día de los Muertos

Good Friday

DECEMBER

Mid-Autumn Festival

Labor Day

All Saints' Day

Rosh Hashanah

Juneteenth

Cinco de Mayo

International Women's Day

Pi Day

Friendship Day

International Talk Like a Pirate Day

Halloween

Valentine's Day

Mother's Day

New Year's Day

Hanukkah

St. Patrick's Day

Winner

You're decorating for the holidays! What's the best decoration?

Wreath

Twinkling Lights

Mistletoe

Tinsel

Holiday Candles

Confetti

Christmas Paintings

Santa Hats

Nutcrackers

Porcelain Elves

Paper Snowflakes

Stickers

Streamers

Balloons

Tree Ornaments

Light-Up Reindeer

Christmas Tree

Stockings

Bells

Candy Canes

Wooden Angels

Cozy Pillows

Kitchen Towels

Pinecones

Gingerbread House

Nativity Scenes

Christmas Gnomes

Train Set

Advent Calendar

Poinsettias

Frosted Trees

Icicles

Winner

What's the best holiday drink?

Eggnog

Chocolate Milk

Mint Hot Chocolate

Candy Cane White Hot Chocolate

Apple Cider

Grape Juice

Sparkling Water

Ginger Ale

Salted Caramel Smoothie

Pumpkin Spice

Lemonade

Iced Tea

Fruit Punch

Vitamin Water

Cherry Limeade

Water

Hot Chocolate

Apple Juice

Blueberry Smoothie

Peppermint Mocha

Cranberry Juice

Apple Pie Punch

Peach Smoothie

Vanilla Milkshake

Chocolate Milkshake

Strawberry Milkshake

Cherry Soda

Watermelon Juice

Orange Juice

Boba Tea

Peanut Butter and Banana Smoothie

Chocolate Malt

Winner

One of these celebrities is coming to Christmas dinner!
Who do you hope it is?

Oprah Winfrey

Taylor Swift

Ariana Grande

Madonna

Michael Jordan

Tom Hanks

Shaquille O'Neal

Justin Bieber

Meghan Trainor

Kim Kardashian

North West

Selena Gomez

Lizzo

Harry Styles

Brie Larson

Chris Hemsworth

Mark Hamill

Harrison Ford

Tom Holland

Zendaya

Cristiano Ronaldo

Kylie Jenner

Beyoncé

LeBron James

Ellen DeGeneres

Bella Hadid

Hailey Bieber

Meghan Markle

Pete Davidson

Lady Gaga

Serena Williams

Michelle Obama

Winner

Every year, Santa gives coal to kids who were naughty. But this year, Santa ran out! What do you think makes the funniest replacement for coal?

Frogs

Eggs

Toenails

Snotty Tissues

Corn Husks

Dog Kibble

Nose Hairs

Grass Clippings

Open Cans of Tuna Fish

Cockroaches

Kitchen Sponges

Toothbrushes

Floss Picks

Moldy Bread

Jellied Moose Noses

Tarantulas

Styrofoam Peanuts

Fake Gold

Whoopee Cushions

Dust Bunnies

Salamanders

Sardines

Melted Ice Cream

Mismatching Socks

Fire Ants

Kombucha

Mushrooms

Reindeer Poop

Dog Toys

Sticks

Ketchup

Dirty Gloves

Winner

What's the best volunteer work to do in honor of Christmas?

Bathe Animals at the Shelter

Work at the Food Bank

Stock Books at the Library

Donate Clothes

Tutor Someone Younger than You

Plant a Tree

Babysit for a Neighbor

Foster a Shelter Animal

Register People to Vote

Fundraise for a Youth Sports Team

Help English Language Learners

Start a Little Library

Clean Up Local Park

Donate Old Toys

Host a Bake Sale

Donate Books

Winner

Work at the Soup Kitchen

Visit Kids at the Hospital

Clean Up the Ocean

Work at the Homeless Center

Write Letters to Seniors

Build a Birdhouse

Work as a Lifeguard

Fundraise for Cancer Patients

Train a Therapy Dog

Sponsor a Family's Christmas Dinner

Knit Scarves for the Homeless

Write to a Pen Pal

Raise Awareness for Mental Health

Host a Garage Sale and Donate the Proceeds

Donate Long Hair

Sweep the Floors of the Library

What's the best holiday smell?

Salted Caramel

Cinnamon

Fir Trees

Peppermint

Eggnog

Sugar Cookies

Crackling Fire

Hot Chocolate

Roses

New Books

S'mores

Pine

Winter Oranges

Roasted Chestnuts

Nutmeg

Maple Syrup

Cedar

Pumpkins

Apple Pies

Vanilla

Hazelnuts

Mistletoe

Honey

Rosemary

Ginger

Figs

Bergamot

Pomegranates

Eucalyptus

Coffee

Mulling Spices

Thyme

Winner

You're getting a new gift for your parent or caretaker!
What do you think they'd like best?

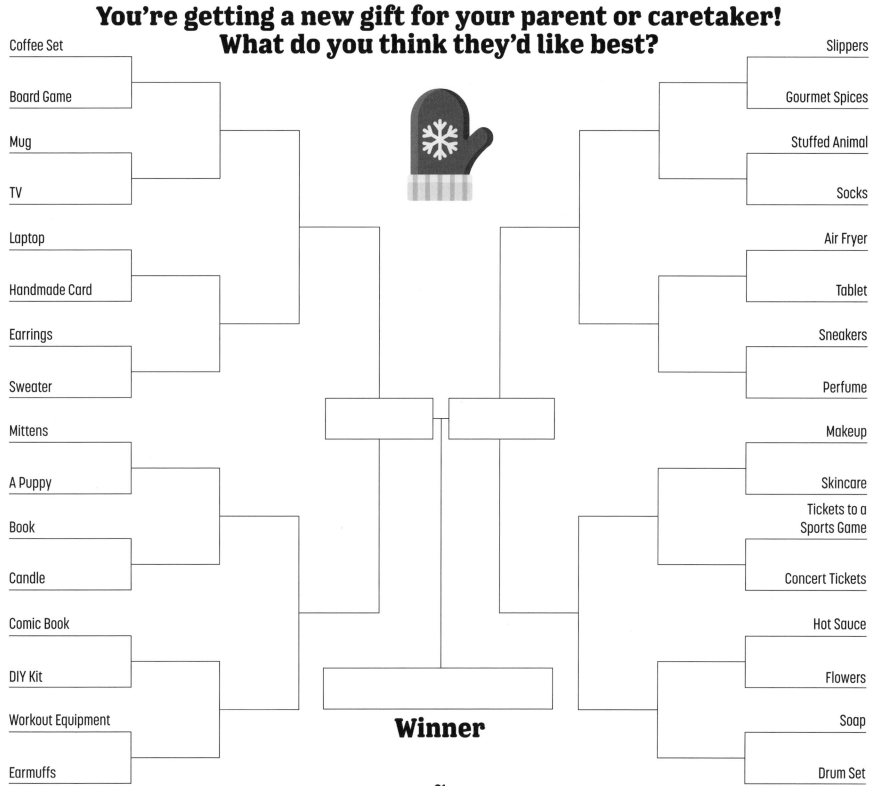

Coffee Set

Board Game

Mug

TV

Laptop

Handmade Card

Earrings

Sweater

Mittens

A Puppy

Book

Candle

Comic Book

DIY Kit

Workout Equipment

Earmuffs

Slippers

Gourmet Spices

Stuffed Animal

Socks

Air Fryer

Tablet

Sneakers

Perfume

Makeup

Skincare

Tickets to a Sports Game

Concert Tickets

Hot Sauce

Flowers

Soap

Drum Set

Winner

Write in your own:

With the following prompt, fill in your own bracketivity!

A family member is giving you a gift card.
What's the best store to get it from?

Winner

Santa's catchphrase is "Ho, ho, ho!" but this year he wants to try something different. What should it be?

No, No, No!

Go, Go, Go!

It's Giving Santa.

Yabba Dabba Gifts!

Reindeer Squad!

Merry Berry!

Slow, Slow, Slow.

To the Santamobile!

Yer a Reindeer, Rudolph.

I'm Santa!

Who Glows There?

Beclaus I Said So.

Treat Yourself!

Welcome to Santatown.

Sleigh.

Santa, Santa, Santa!

Snow, Snow, Snow.

Suit Up!

Don't Make Me Take out the Claus.

Soot Yourself.

Your Presents is Requested.

Oh Deer!

Fir Sure.

Told You Snow.

Don't Be Elfish.

It's Snow Time!

Santa Forever!

Glow, Glow, Glow!

Let it Rein!

Fingers and Mistletoes!

Cookie Dough!

Oh My Santa!

Winner

You're getting a musical instrument for the holidays!
What is it?

Piano

Acoustic Guitar

Ukulele

Saxophone

Violin

Bagpipes

Harmonica

Banjo

Gong

French Horn

Piccolo

Harp

Bongos

Recorder

Drum Set

Cello

Trumpet

Clarinet

Flute

Mandolin

Oboe

Tuba

Bassoon

Tambourine

Xylophone

Melodica

Electric Guitar

Fiddle

Accordion

Cymbals

Ocarina

Trombone

Winner

What's the best holiday story or book?

The Polar Express

Bracketivity Holiday

How the Grinch Stole Christmas

Rudolph the Red-Nosed Reindeer

The Elf on the Shelf

"The Elves and the Shoemaker"

A Christmas Carol

"The Nutcracker and the Mouse King"

A Charlie Brown Christmas

How to Catch a Snowman

The Night Before Christmas

Strega Nona

The Snowy Day

The Velveteen Rabbit

Li'l Rabbit's Kwanzaa

Where's Waldo? Santa Spectacular

"The Little Match Girl"

"Little Piccola"

"The Gingerbread Man"

The Other Wise Man

"The Gift of the Magi"

The Giving Tree

Bear Stays Up for Christmas

How to Catch an Elf

I Spy Christmas

Pig the Elf

Dear Santa

"The Twelve Days of Christmas"

The Girl Who Saved Christmas

The Itsy Bitsy Snowman

Polar Bear, Polar Bear, What Do You See?

The Wonky Donkey

Winner

Which person from history would you most like to share a holiday cookie with?

Amelia Earhart

John F. Kennedy

Abraham Lincoln

Cleopatra

Queen Victoria

George Washington

Aristotle

Julius Caesar

William Shakespeare

Mahatma Gandhi

Ada Lovelace

Vincent van Gogh

Joan of Arc

Isaac Newton

Benjamin Franklin

Marilyn Monroe

Leonardo da Vinci

Thomas Edison

Alexander Hamilton

Edgar Allan Poe

Elvis Presley

Sacagawea

Jane Austen

Rosa Parks

Mother Teresa

King Tutankhamen

Vlad the Impaler

Anne Boleyn

Marie Antoinette

Anastasia Romanov

Martin Luther King Jr.

Stephen Hawking

Winner

It's ugly sweater time!
What's on the ugliest sweater that you can think of?

Ducks

Radioactive Ducks

Teenage Santa

Elves

Frankenstein

Tacky Reindeer

Gnomes

Santa Doing Yoga

Candy Canes

Cats, also in Sweaters

Dinosaurs

Giant Bow

Tinsel

3-D Reindeer Antlers

Fruitcake

Photo of Family

Teddy Bears

Cheesy Saying

A Celebrity

Dog Butts

Fish

Cartoon Ogre

Fairies

Mountains

3-D String Lights

Cheeseburgers

Velvet Hearts

Snowflake Pattern

Vampires

Christmas Trees

Tacos

Mutant Tacos

Winner

What's the best sport to play or partake in during the holidays?

Ice Skating

Tennis

Golf

Snowboarding

Horse Racing

Volleyball

Swimming

Badminton

Bobsleighing

Skiing

Soccer

Boxing

Table Tennis

Roller Skating

Cricket

Ice Hockey

Rock Climbing

Archery

Skateboarding

Fencing

Kickboxing

Scuba Diving

Taekwondo

Bowling

Football

Basketball

Water Skiing

Darts

Karate

Fishing

Cheerleading

Snowball Fighting

Winner

Santa is bringing you a pet for Christmas!
Which pet will it be?

Porcupine

Guinea Pig

Rat

Iguana

Dog

Cat

Horse

Bearded Dragon

Fox

Capybara

Turtle

Raccoon

Tarantula

Hermit Crab

Goldfish

Toad

Parrot

Goat

Hedgehog

Chinchilla

Sugar Glider

Skunk

Squirrel Monkey

Donkey

Peacock

Parakeet

Python

Axolotl

Scorpion

Gecko

Ferret

Armadillo

Winner

Which of these characters would help you set up the nicest Christmas tree?

Superman

Bugs Bunny

Captain America

Darth Vader

Joker

Spider-Man

Fred Flinstone

Alice in Wonderland

Goku

Peter Pan

Charlie Brown

Wonder Woman

Robin Hood

Scooby-Doo

Popeye

She-Hulk

Spongebob Squarepants

Winnie-the-Pooh

Optimus Prime

Rey Skywalker

Godzilla

Forrest Gump

E.T.

Mario

Mary Poppins

Ash Ketchum

Sonic the Hedgehog

Cinderella

Sherlock Holmes

T'challa

The Mad Hatter

The Wicked Witch of the West

Winner

It's Christmas morning!
What's the best breakfast food?

Yogurt Parfait

Quiche Lorraine

Cinnamon Rolls

Chicken Apple Sausage

Pumpkin Pancakes

French Toast

Pecan Pie

Ham and Cheese Omelet

Gingerbread Muffins

Frittata

Vanilla Scone

Cream Cheese Danish

Bagel and Cream Cheese

Chocolate Pancakes

Blueberry Waffles

Biscuits with Butter

Breakfast Tacos

Oatmeal

Poached Eggs

Breakfast Sandwich

Toaster Strudel

Hashbrowns

Sticky Buns

Breakfast Burritos

Peppermint Chocolate Doughnuts

Christmas Cookies

Scrambled Eggs

Banana Pudding

Fruit Tart

Smoked Salmon

Red Velvet Pancakes

Coffee Cake

Winner

Write in your own:

With the following prompt, fill in your own bracketivity!

Which friend of yours would LOVE to get a whoopee cushion for Christmas?

Winner

What's a gift you'd really like to receive?

Dollhouse

New Clothes

Video Game System

Soap

Candles

Mug

Slippers

Gift Card

Laptop

Tablet

Poetry Books

Comic Books

Saxophone

Pajamas

Fuzzy Socks

Gold Necklace

Bicycle

TV

Golf Club

Bubble Bath Kit

Yoga Mat

Drum Set

Keyboard

Kitten

Ice Skates

Throw Pillows

Weighted Blanket

Stuffed Animal

Sunglasses

Headphones

Sneakers

Plants

Winner

What's a gift you'd return immediately?
(Hint: It's like the last Bracketivity, but in reverse!)

Dollhouse

New Clothes

Video Game System

Soap

Candles

Mug

Slippers

Gift Card

Laptop

Tablet

Poetry Books

Comic Books

Saxophone

Pajamas

Fuzzy Socks

Gold Necklace

Bicycle

TV

Golf Club

Bubble Bath Kit

Yoga Mat

Drum Set

Keyboard

Kitten

Ice Skates

Throw Pillows

Weighted Blanket

Stuffed Animal

Sunglasses

Headphones

Sneakers

Plants

Winner

What's the best holiday candy or sweet?

Peanut Butter Fudge

Chocolate Truffles

Pumpkin Pecan Bars

Peanut Brittle

Jelly Doughnuts

Candied Pecans

Candy Canes

Bubble Gum

Peppermint Bark

Popcorn Balls

Chocolate Pretzels

Marshmallows

Macaroons

Gummy Bears

Chocolate Turtles

Candied Oranges

Gumdrops

Toffee

Saltwater Taffy

Chocolate Santas

Hazelnut Truffles

Meringues

Chocolate-Covered Strawberries

Candy Apple

Lollipops

Biscotti

Jellybeans

Pralines

Kettle Corn

Licorice

Chocolate Coins

Marzipan

Winner

Santa is getting a new reindeer!
What should its name be?

Dancer

Waffles

Yankee

Aphrodite

Gus

Thunder

Singer

Flinger

Finger

Thor

Loki

Arbiter

Chaos

Sandra

Cole

Meteor

Glider

Climber

Lady

Marshmallow

Fluffy

Rooney

Max

Pickles

Frankie

Holly

Noelle

Natalie

Jumper

Spinner

Zeus

Skipper

Winner

Think about these places in your neighborhood. Where is the best place to see holiday lights or decor?

My Place!

Neighbor's Home

School

Indoor Mall

Community Center

Grocery Store

Best Friend's Home

Christmas Fair

Toy Store

Library

Community Pool

Airport

Outdoor Mall

Neighborhood Drive

Post Office

Clothing Store

Movie Theater

Hospital

Museum

Park

Train Station

Coffee Shop

Shoe Store

Fire Department

Church

Beach

Book Store

Arcade

Restaurant

Ice-Skating Rink

Garden

Theme Park

Winner

Which of these people in your life would most like to receive a puppy from Santa?

Mom

Grandpa

Best Friend's Parent

Kindergarten Teacher

School Principal

Restaurant Worker

Cousin

Uncle

Sibling

Other Sibling

Sports Coach

Music Teacher

Religious Leader

Closest Neighbor

Vice Principal

Librarian

(If this person, i.e. a sports coach, isn't in your life, fill in with a friend's name instead! Just don't double up.)

Mail Delivery Person

Younger Family Member

Oldest Family Member

Dentist

Therapist or Counselor

Firefighter or Police Officer

Babysitter

Musician

Bus Driver

Retail Worker

Art Teacher

Grandma

Dad

Aunt

Current Teacher

Best Friend

Winner

Which of these people in your life would most like to receive new socks from Santa?

Mom

Grandpa

Best Friend's Parent

Kindergarten Teacher

School Principal

Restaurant Worker

Cousin

Uncle

Sibling

Other Sibling

Sports Coach

Music Teacher

Religious Leader

Closest Neighbor

Vice Principal

Librarian

(If this person, i.e. a sports coach, isn't in your life, fill in with a friend's name instead! Just don't double up.)

Mail Delivery Person

Younger Family Member

Oldest Family Member

Dentist

Therapist or Counselor

Firefighter or Police Officer

Babysitter

Musician

Bus Driver

Retail Worker

Art Teacher

Grandma

Dad

Aunt

Current Teacher

Best Friend

Winner

Which of these people in your life would most like to receive a new book from Santa?

Mom

Grandpa

Best Friend's Parent

Kindergarten Teacher

School Principal

Restaurant Worker

Cousin

Uncle

Sibling

Other Sibling

Sports Coach

Music Teacher

Religious Leader

Closest Neighbor

Vice Principal

Librarian

(If this person, i.e. a sports coach, isn't in your life, fill in with a friend's name instead! Just don't double up.)

Winner

Mail Delivery Person

Younger Family Member

Oldest Family Member

Dentist

Therapist or Counselor

Firefighter or Police Officer

Babysitter

Musician

Bus Driver

Retail Worker

Art Teacher

Grandma

Dad

Aunt

Current Teacher

Best Friend

Which of these people in your life would most like to receive a new computer from Santa?

Mom

Grandpa

Best Friend's Parent

Kindergarten Teacher

School Principal

Restaurant Worker

Cousin

Uncle

Sibling

Other Sibling

Sports Coach

Music Teacher

Religious Leader

Closest Neighbor

Vice Principal

Librarian

(If this person, i.e. a sports coach, isn't in your life, fill in with a friend's name instead! Just don't double up.)

Mail Delivery Person

Younger Family Member

Oldest Family Member

Dentist

Therapist or Counselor

Firefighter or Police Officer

Babysitter

Musician

Bus Driver

Retail Worker

Art Teacher

Grandma

Dad

Aunt

Current Teacher

Best Friend

Winner

Write in your own:

With the following prompt, fill in your own bracketivity!

What's the book you'd MOST like to receive for the holidays? (It doesn't have to be a holiday book.) Write in 32 answers, then fill it out!

Winner

Write in your own:

With the following prompt, fill in your own bracketivity!

What's the movie you'd MOST like to see on Christmas? (It doesn't have to be a Christmas movie.) Write in 32 answers, then fill it out!

Winner

What's the best part of New Year's celebrations?

Wearing Something Sparkly

Hosting a Party

Drinking Grape Juice

Counting Down to Midnight

Eating Snacks

Making Food

Blowing into a Noisemaker

Cheering at Midnight

Being off from School

Wearing Party Hats

Being with Friends

Playing Video Games

Taking Photos

Hosting Karaoke

Watching TV

Making a Time Capsule

Staying up Late

Playing Board Games

Reading a Book

Using Glowsticks

Eating Fondue

Watching a Movie

Making a Video

Having a Snowball Fight

Stargazing

Being with Family

Singing

Dancing

Throwing Confetti

Making Resolutions

Watching Fireworks

Attending a Party

Winner

Of these, which design or pattern would you most like to wear on your holiday pajamas?

Black and White

Red and Green

Cheetah Print

Pink

Sparkly

Lace

Tie Dye

Buffalo Check

Polka Dots

Fuzzy

Blue

Striped

Knitted

Embroidered

With my Favorite Saying

Santa

Crochet

Favorite Cartoon

Snowflake

Reindeer

Cats

Chevrons

Geometric

Checkered

Rainbow

Green

Floral

Giraffe Print

Cow Print

Ugly

Leather

Zebra Print

Winner

Which fictional villain is the naughtiest?

The Joker

The Wicked Witch of the West

The Evil Queen

Count Dracula

Kylo Ren

Scar

Emperor Palpatine

Hannibal Lecter

Captain Hook

Lex Luthor

The White Witch

Mother Gothel

Queen of Hearts

Yzma

Loki

Doctor Doom

Gollum

Bellatrix Lestrange

Green Goblin

Mysterio

The Grinch

Lord Farquaad

Jafar

Harley Quinn

Ursula

Maleficent

Saruman

Bane

Thanos

Lord Voldemort

Cruella De Vil

Darth Vader

Winner

What's the best gift to bring to a white elephant exchange?

Action Figure

Dog Toy

Chocolate Bar

Fluffy Pillow

Blanket

Computer Keyboard

Slippers

Keychain

Video Game

Headphones

Deck of Cards

Comic Book

Pet Rock

Gardening Supplies

Nail Polish

Candy

Waffle Maker

Notebook

Wall Calendar

Mug

Toothbrush

Cookbook

Pizza Cutter

Speakers

Popcorn Machine

Boardgame

Ramen Bowl

Funny Magnets

Phone Case

Stuffed Animal

Historical Book

Mittens

Winner

Which Thanksgiving food or drink wins?

Sweet Potatoes

Dinner Rolls

Turkey

Ham

Mac and Cheese

Lasagna

Mashed Potatoes

Roasted Squash

Creamed Spinach

Roasted Corn

Gravy

Pecan Pie

Candied Yams

Cornbread

Butternut Squash Soup

Sweet Potato Pie

Apple Cider

Strawberry Rhubarb Pie

Carrot Cake

Pumpkin Cheesecake

Cheese Plate

Spinach-Artichoke Dip

Glazed Carrots

Vegetarian Roast

Shortbread

Hot Chocolate

Apple Pie

Pumpkin Pie

Cranberry Sauce

Brussel Sprouts

Green Beans

Stuffing

Winner

Of these places, which is your favorite to shop for holiday presents?

Walmart

Barnes & Noble

Five Below

Dollar Tree

Amazon

Apple

Macy's

Costco

Sears

T.J. Maxx

Marshalls

Kmart

FAO Schwarz

H&M

Gap

Nike

Winner

Hot Topic

GameStop

Hallmark

JCPenney

Adidas

Toys "R" Us

eBay

Bath & Body Works

American Eagle

Ross

Nordstrom

Big Lots

Kohl's

Best Buy

Sephora

Target

For the holidays, you received an all-expenses paid trip! Of these, which country would you most like to visit?

Mexico

Indonesia

Ireland

Australia

France

Switzerland

Egypt

China

Brazil

Japan

Kenya

Madagascar

New Zealand

United States

Canada

Syria

South Korea

Romania

Greece

Pakistan

Croatia

South Africa

Norway

Germany

Philippines

United Kingdom

Poland

Italy

Turkey

Morocco

India

Peru

Winner

There's a new holiday movie on TV! Who do you hope plays the lead?

Leonardo DiCaprio

Tom Hanks

Brad Pitt

Morgan Freeman

Taylor Swift

Samuel L. Jackson

Chris Pratt

Robert Downey Jr.

Florence Pugh

Emma Watson

Letitia Wright

Gal Gadot

Ryan Reynolds

Lupita Nyong'o

Benedict Wong

Lindsay Lohan

Winner

Jason Momoa

Chris Evans

Scarlett Johansson

Margot Robbie

Simu Liu

Elizabeth Olsen

Jojo Siwa

Adam Driver

Daisy Ridley

John Boyega

Natalie Portman

Oscar Isaac

Daniel Radcliffe

Harry Styles

Brie Larson

Selena Gomez

Write in your own:

With the following prompt, fill in your own bracketivity!

Think about all your ornaments.
Which one is the best? Write them in
the 32 choices on the sides. Then,
find out which one would win!

Winner

You're going to a friend's house for Hanukkah. What are you most excited for?

Eating Latkes (Potato Pancakes)

Lighting Candles

Saying Prayers

Listening to Stories

Singing

Doing Mitzvot (Volunteer Work)

Eating Gelt (Chocolate Coins)

Giving Presents

Learning about Hanukkah

Making Latkes (Potato Pancakes)

Being with Friends

Watching Hanukkah Movies

Wrapping Presents

Meeting Other Family Members

Eating Brisket

Making Challah (Bread)

Dancing

Drinking Grape Juice

Seeing the Hanukkah Lights

Eating Fried Food

Reading Hanukkah Books

Learning Some Hebrew

Watching Others Dance

Eating Rugelach (Pastries)

Eating Challah (Bread)

Making Doughnuts

Going to Synagogue

Decorating

Getting Presents

Listening to Music

Eating Doughnuts

Playing Dreidel

Winner

What's the best décor to have on a holiday card?

Family Photo

Santa

Plaid

Pie

Snowman

Pumpkins

Christmas Tree

Reindeer

Ornaments

Penguin

Kinara

Ice Skates

Snow Globe

Nativity Scene

Presents

Quote

Puppies

Kittens

Camel

Cookies

Fireplace

Wreath

Elves

Christmas Lights

Mrs. Claus

Santa's Sleigh

Hot Chocolate

Fruitcake

Bowtie

Photo of Me

Mittens

Gingerbread House

Winner

54

Now it's your turn!

You're a pro at Bracketivities, especially holiday ones. Santa would be proud of you! Turn the page and make your own. You can also use this page to jot down any notes you have.

Winner

Winner

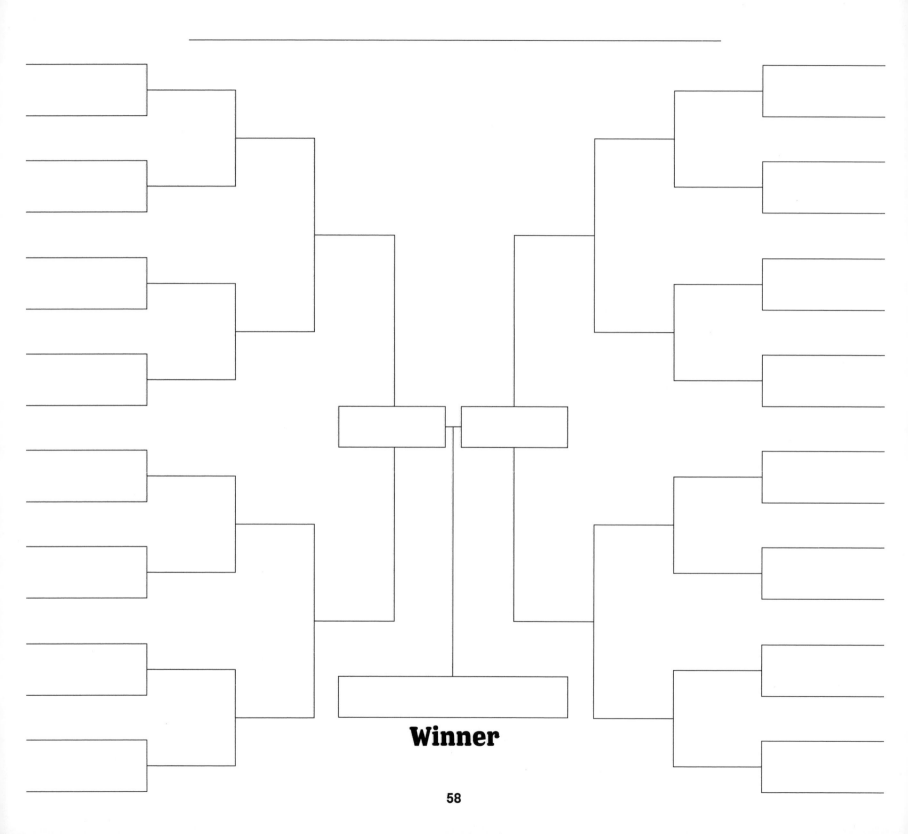

Winner

Winner

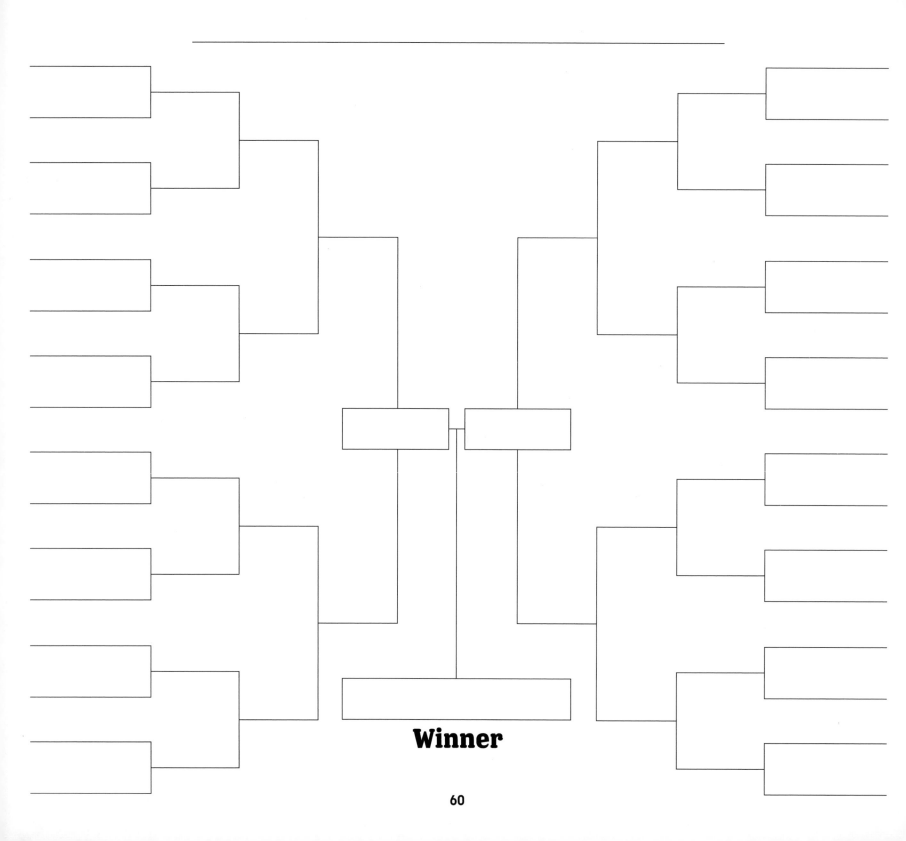

Winner

Winner

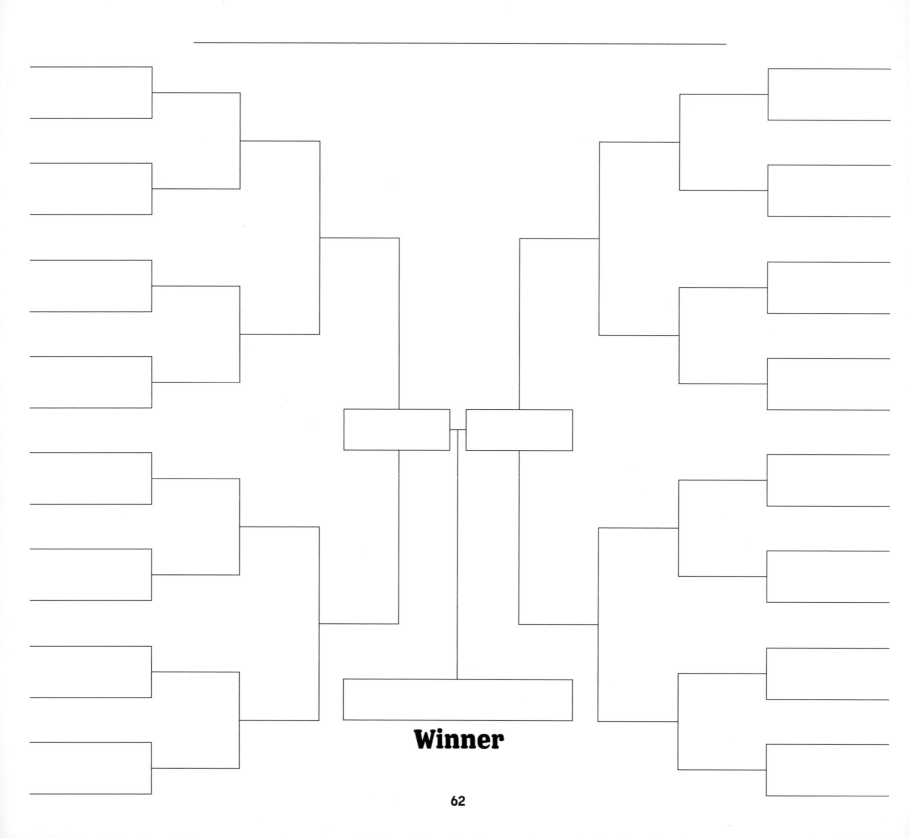

Winner

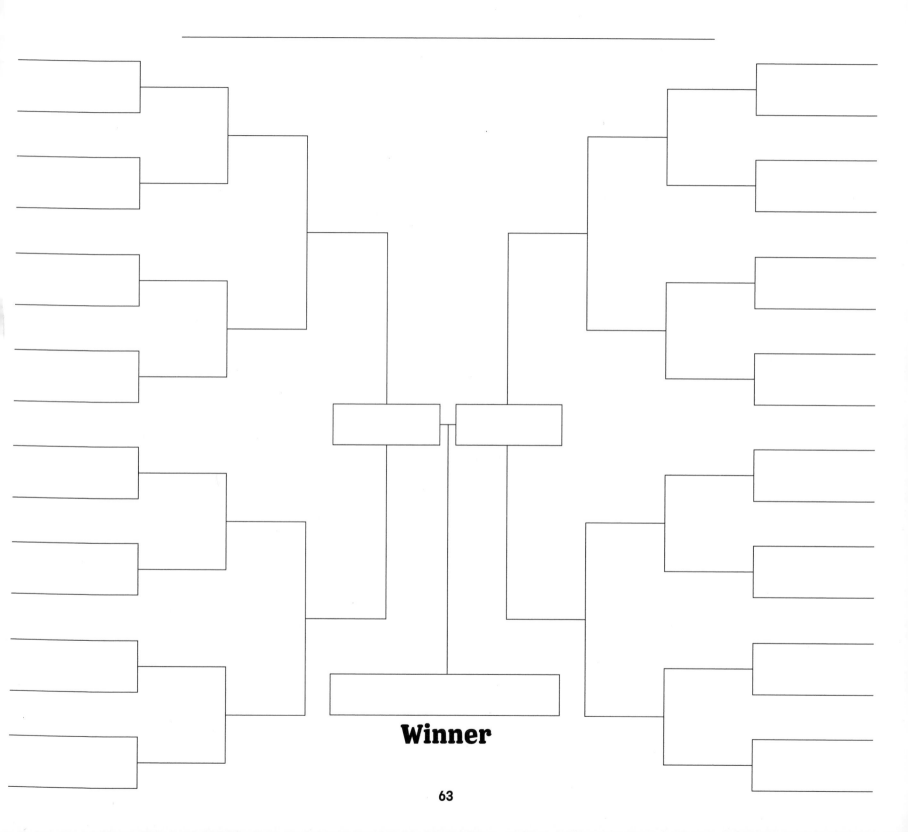

Winner

Winner